LAWS

Zachary A. Kelly

The Rourke Corporation, Inc.
Vero Beach, Florida 32964

PHOTO CREDITS:
Tony Gray: pages 6, 7, 22, 24, 36, 36, 39, 42; East Coast Studios: pages 9, 16, 20, 44; Danny Bachelor: cover, pages 17, 32, 34, 37; © U.S. Secret Service: pages 26, 27; © Reuters/Lou Dematteis/Archive Photos: page 19; © Reuters/Blake Sell/Archive Photos: page 29; unknown: pages 12, 14

PRODUCED BY: East Coast Studios, Merritt Island, Florida

EDITORIAL SERVICES:
Penworthy Learning Systems

Library of Congress Cataloging-in-Publication Data

Kelly, Zachary A., 1970-
    Laws / by Zachary A. Kelly.
        p. cm. — (Law and order)
    Summary: An overview of the American legal system, including why laws are necessary, how they are made, criminal and civil law, law enforcement, and the rights of victims and of the accused.
        ISBN 0-86593-573-4
    1. Justice, Administration of—United States—Juvenile literature. 2. Legislation—United States—Juvenile literature. [1. Law. 2. Justice, Administration of.] I. Title. II. Series.
KF8700.Z9K4   1999
340—DC21   98-6023
                                                                       CIP
                                                                       AC

Printed in the USA

TABLE OF CONTENTS

The Constitution

We the People of the United States, in Order to form a more perfect Union, establish Justic Tranquility, provide for the common Defence, promote the general Welfare, and secure the Blessings of Liberty to ourselves and our Poster tablish this CONSTITUTION for the United States of America.

Article. I.

...TION 1. All legislative Powers herein granted shall be vested in a Congress of the United States, which shall consist of a Senate and Ho tives.

...TION 2. The House of Representatives shall be composed of Members chosen every second Year by the People of the several States, and State shall have the Qualifications requisite for Electors of the most numerous Branch of the State Legislature.

No Person shall be a Representative who shall not have attained to the Age of twenty-five Years, and been seven Years a Citizen of the who shall not, when elected, be an Inhabitant of that State in which he shall be chosen.

[Representatives and direct Taxes shall be apportioned among the several States which may be included within this Union, according to ...bers, which shall be determined by adding to the whole Number of free Persons, including those bound to Service for a Term of Years, and taxed, three fifths of all other Persons.] The actual Enumeration shall be made within three Years after the first Meeting of the Congress o within every subsequent Term of ten Years, in such Manner as they shall by Law direct. The Number of Representatives shall not exceed ...usand, but each State shall have at Least one Representative; and until such enumeration shall be made, the State of New Hampshire shal ...se three, Massachusetts eight, Rhode-Island and Providence Plantations one, Connecticut five, New-York six, New Jersey four, Pennsylva ...e, Maryland six, Virginia ten, North Carolina five, South Carolina five, and Georgia three.

When vacancies happen in the Representation from any State, the Executive Authority thereof shall issue Writs of Election to fill such The House of Representatives shall chuse their Speaker and other Officers; and shall have the sole Power of Impeachment.

...ECTION 3. The Senate of the United States shall be composed of two Senators from each State, chosen by the Legislature thereof, for si ...enator shall have one Vote.

Immediately after they shall be assembled in Consequence of the first Election, they shall be divided as equally as may be into three ...f the Senators of the first Class shall be vacated at the Expiration of the second Year, of the second Class at the Expiration of the fourth Y ...Class at the Expiration of the sixth Year, so that one-third may be chosen every second Year; and if Vacancies happen by Resignation, or o ...Recess of the Legislature of any State, the Executive thereof may make temporary Appointments until the next Meeting of the Legislature, u ...such Vacancies.

No Person shall be a Senator who shall not have attained to the Age of thirty Years, and been nine Years a Citizen of the United St ...not, when elected, be an Inhabitant of that State for which he shall be chosen.

The Vice President of the United States shall be President of the Senate, but shall have no Vote, unless they be equally divided. The Senate shall chuse their other Officers, and also a President pro tempore, in the absence of the Vice President, or when he sh ...of President of the United States.

The Senate shall have the sole Power to try all Impeachments. When sitting for that Purpose, they shall be on Oath or Affirmation. the United States is tried, the Chief Justice shall preside: And no Person shall be convicted without the Concurrence of two thirds of the

Judgment in Cases of Impeachment shall not extend further than to removal from Office, and disqualification to hold and enjoy any ...or Profit under the United States: but the Party convicted shall nevertheless be liable and subject to Indictment, Trial, Judgment and Pun

...Law. SECTION 4. The Times, Places and Manner of holding Elections for Senators and Representatives, shall be prescribed in each State ...of; but the Congress may at any time by Law make or alter such Regulations, except as to the Place of Chusing Senators.

The Congress shall assemble at least once in every Year, and such Meeting shall be on the first Monday in December, unless the ...a different Day.

SECTION 5. Each House shall be the Judge of the Elections, Returns and Qualifications of its own Members, and a Majority of each to do Business; but a smaller number may adjourn from day to day, and may be authorized to compel the Attendance of absent Members, such Penalties as each House may provide.

Each House may determine the Rules of its Proceedings, punish its Members for disorderly Behavior, and, with the Concurrence ...Member.

Each House shall keep a Journal of its Proceedings, and from time to time publish the same, excepting such Parts as may in th ...crecy; and the Yeas and Nays of the Members of either House on any question shall, at the Desire of one fifth of those Present, be ent

Neither House, during the Session of Congress, shall, without the Consent of the other, adjourn for more than three days, nor ...in which the two Houses shall be sitting.

SECTION 6. The Senators and Representatives shall receive a Compensation for their Services, to be ascertained by Law, and pai United States. They shall in all Cases, except Treason, Felony and Breach of the Peace, be privileged from Arrest during their Atten ...Houses, and in going to and returning from the same; and for any Speech or Debate in either House, they shall not be ques ...during the Time for which he was elected, be appointed to any civil Office under the Auth ...been encreased during such time; and no Person holding any O

A copy of the U.S. Constitution

CHAPTER ONE

THE NEED FOR LAW AND ORDER

Why do we need laws? One important reason is that laws protect peoples' *rights.* Our Declaration of Independence says that all people have the right to life, liberty, and the pursuit of happiness. Laws are made so that everybody gets to use these rights.

Laws set the limits of what we can do without hurting others or ourselves. Within these limits, we can do whatever we want as we live our lives. The limits set by law help keep others from violating our rights.

A policeman takes a statement from a possible crime victim.

Laws give us rules to follow. These rules help us know if our rights have been violated. Every time a law is broken, somebody's rights are violated.

We need laws to settle conflicts between people. Sometimes people do wrong to others when they disagree. When this happens, laws help us decide who is right and who is wrong.

Disobeying speed limits violates the law.

Then, we need laws that tell us how to punish the wrongdoer. Laws tell us how to repay the people who are harmed in some way. Laws help us carry out the idea of **justice**, or fairness, in conflicts. Justice happens three ways. Justice is done when we decide who is right and who is wrong. Justice happens when wrongdoers pay for their actions. Justice is done when wronged people are paid back. Laws bring order by giving us rules that everybody can understand and follow.

Law & Order Facts

Law and order exist for the purpose of establishing justice and . . . when they fail in this purpose they become the dangerously structured dams that block the flow of social progress.—Martin Luther King, Jr. (1929-1968)

Laws against speeding in school zones helps keep the children safe.

Knowing and following the rules leads to *predictability.* People can make choices easily when they can predict what the result will be. When you see a car coming toward you on the road, for example, you predict it will either go around you or stop, before it hits you. If you couldn't predict the driver's action you would have to jump out of the way to make sure you would not be hit. A society without predictable rules—laws—would be in a similar state of disorder, always jumping to avoid something bad.

CHAPTER TWO

MAKING LAWS

The United States Congress is the part of our government that makes laws for our country. Two groups of lawmakers make up Congress. One group is called the House of Representatives; the other is called the Senate. This system of two groups in Congress is called a **bicameral** system. In a bicameral system the two groups must agree on the laws they make, which helps them make laws that arc fair.

Not all laws are made by Congress, though. Each state in the U.S makes laws about certain things in that state.

Governments create the laws that protect us.

Each state has its own bicameral system, called the *state legislature.* A local group can also make laws that apply only to a county, city, or town.

Laws are made in three steps. First, a lawmaker comes up with an idea for a law—a way to solve a problem or meet a need in society. Then, the idea is written as a **bill**, a request for a law. (Many bills are talked about in Congress and state legislatures every year.) Then, the lawmakers vote on the bill to decide if they want it to become a law.

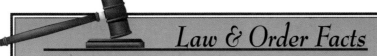

If the majority votes for the bill, it becomes a new law. If the majority votes against the bill, it does not become a law and is dropped.

How do lawmakers know if they should vote for or against a bill? They are elected by citizens to make laws that the people want. Before voting on a bill, lawmakers talk to some of these people. Lawmakers often vote as the people say, though they do not have to. Lawmakers listen to the people and vote to represent the majority.

This process is called *representing* the people. By representing the people, a lawmaker helps make laws that most people want.

Lawmakers in Washington create our federal laws.

CHAPTER THREE

How Laws Protect Us

Laws protect us from violations of our rights. If our rights are violated, where can we go and who can we ask for help? For help we often go to law enforcement officers. The local and state police and the FBI are law enforcement officers. For help when rights are violated, we can go to our system of **courts**. People who make up the court decide whether rights have been violated. They do this by listening to and looking at what happened to a person before he or she came to the court for help. If his or her rights have been violated, courts have the power to punish the violator.

Several types of law enforcement help us with many public needs.

Courts use two kinds of laws to decide whether someone's rights have been violated: criminal or civil law.

Criminal law is used mainly in cases of violent crime. Violent crime is one that violates a person's basic rights. For example, hurting someone on purpose or stealing are violent crimes. In court, a judge decides whether a person is guilty of a crime, after listening to all the facts. If a person is **convicted**, or found guilty, then he or she is given a sentence.

A police officer testifies in a court of law.

A sentence is the penalty a criminal must pay for a crime, such as time in jail, a fine, and/or community service.

Civil law deals with non-violent crimes. Civil law often deals with family problems, like divorce. Conflicts over money and contracts are settled through civil law. If a person refuses to pay a debt, he or she can be sued in civil court. A person who is sued must go to court and then do whatever the court decides.

One of our most important rights protected by law is the right to protest.

Criminal law has one goal: convict wrongdoers. Civil law, though, deals with many different problems. In civil law, many situations are unclear. Sometimes even the rights of the person sued and the person suing in court are not clear. One goal of civil law is to decide the rights of both of them. Another goal is to award money to the person who has been wronged.

CHAPTER FOUR

WHEN LAWS ARE BROKEN

What happens when somebody breaks a law? First, the person is **arrested** which means a law enforcement officer charges him or her with a crime. Then the officer takes the person to the local jail. The accused person must stay in jail until he or she is given a *first appearance.* Everybody charged must have a first appearance within 24 hours of being arrested.

Someone suspected of a crime must be arrested before going to court.

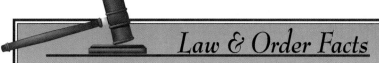

In a first appearance, the person goes before a judge in court. The judge decides how much the person must pay for **bail**. Bail is money paid to the court to let an arrested person out of jail until he or she goes to trial. If the person does not pay bail, he or she must stay in jail until it's time to go to court again.

The second time an accused person goes to court is called the *arraignment.* During the arraignment the person tells the judge whether he or she is innocent or guilty. This statement is called the **plea**. Sometimes the person tells the judge that he or she is guilty. If that happens, the judge usually sentences the person right then. Sometimes a person will tell the judge "not guilty." Then the judge must decide if the person is telling the truth. An accused person can refuse to plead guilty or not guilty. This plea is called **no contest**. The court usually decides that a person who pleads "no contest" is guilty.

When a person claims to be innocent, he or she must go to trial. There are two kinds of trials: In a bench trial, a judge listens to the evidence for and against the accused person and decides whether the person is guilty or innocent. In a jury trial a group of citizens listen to the evidence and decides whether the accused person is guilty or innocent. If a judge or a jury says the person is innocent, he or she goes free. If the person is found guilty, then he or she is sentenced by the judge.

CHAPTER FIVE

FEDERAL LAWS

The U.S. has a *federal* form of government. A federal government is divided into parts that work together. One part, the *central* government, makes laws for the entire country. Another part, state governments, makes laws for each state. Local governments make laws in small areas of states, such as *counties* and *cities*. The central government cannot control the state or local governments, but it can pass laws that states must follow.

Federal agents help ensure that federal laws are obeyed.

Everybody in the country must follow federal laws, made by the central government. If people break a federal law, they can be arrested and taken to the nearest jail. When they go to court, though, they go to **federal court**. Federal court is a special part of the court system. Federal court deals with violations of federal laws. If a person is convicted by a federal court, he or she may be sent to a federal prison. (People who break state or local laws may be sent to a state prison.)

Federal agents make an arrest. Making counterfeit, or fake, money is a federal crime.

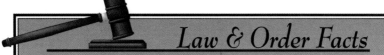

The first federal laws were written in our *Constitution.* The people who organized our country wrote the Constitution to establish the rights of people (individual and states). Another reason for the Constitution was to set limits on the federal government. Rights have been added in the form of **amendments**. The Constitution now has 27 amendments. The first amendments assured the freedom to speak or otherwise express, publish, gather, and worship as one chooses. The thirteenth amendment made slavery illegal in 1865. The Constitution is our most basic set of laws. All other laws are based on them.

These protesters avoid breaking the law by having a peaceful demonstration.

A California corrections officer inspects the plans of a new state facility.

CHAPTER SIX

State and Local Laws

State laws are made in each state and apply only to the state that made them. If a lawbreaker is caught, he or she can be **extradited** (taken back to the state where the law was broken). Once there, he or she will be taken to state court to be judged. Every state has its own court system, which is separate from the federal court system. A person convicted in a state court can sometimes **appeal** to federal court.

A small county courthouse

To appeal means to ask a higher court to decide the case again. Every accused person has the right to appeal.

Counties usually make local laws. Cities and towns also make local laws. If a person breaks a local law, he or she goes to state court. A state court decides both local and state cases. People who break local laws also have the right to appeal. They usually must appeal to the state supreme court before they can appeal to a federal court. The state supreme court is the most powerful court in the state.

Why do we need state and local laws along with the federal laws that apply to all of us? Some laws that may be necessary in one state may not make sense in another. For example, a law in Michigan against ice skating on public ponds would be useless in Florida. State and local laws help people manage situations where they live, without violating the rights of people in other places.

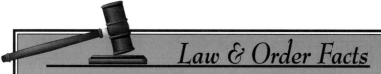

Law & Order Facts

Let reverence for the laws be breathed by every American mother to the lisping babe that prattles on her lap. Let it be taught in schools, in seminaries, and in colleges.— Abraham Lincoln (1809-1865)

The judge is always in charge of a courtroom. The courtroom is often referred to as his or her courtroom.

CHAPTER SEVEN

RIGHTS OF THE ACCUSED

Our legal system gives rights to people accused of crimes. These rights make sure that people are treated fairly, even if they are guilty. An accused person is *presumed* (thought to be) *innocent until proven guilty.* A judge or jury must presume the person is innocent until the evidence makes them change their minds. Sometimes people are accused wrongly. The right of presumed innocence protects them.

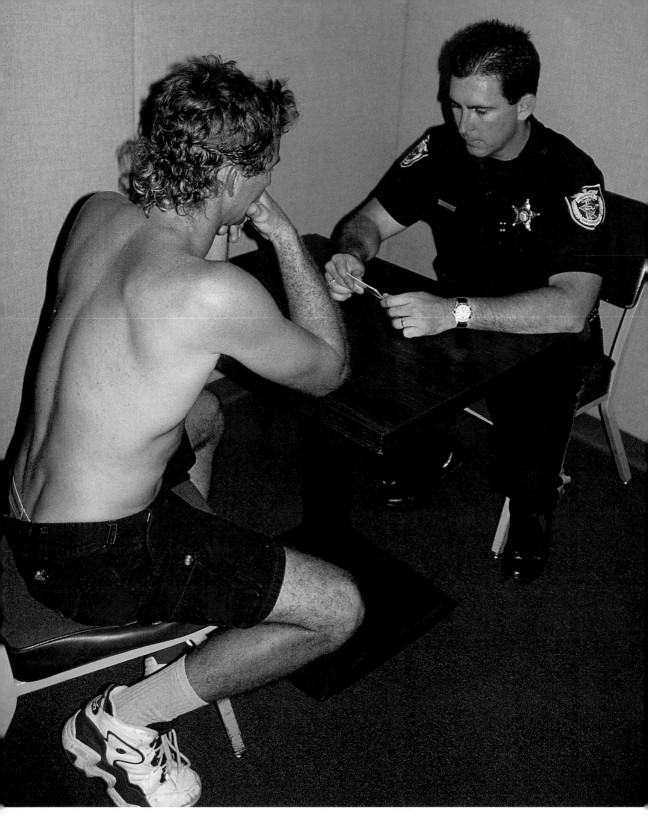

A police officer reads the Miranda rights to a suspect.

When a person is arrested, he or she is told of three rights, called the **Miranda rights**. The arresting officer says, "You have the right to remain silent." The arrested person does not have to say anything that might prove his or her guilt. The arresting officer says, "Anything you say can and will be used against you in a court of law." The person's own words when told to the judge or jury may cause them to decide the person is guilty. The arresting officer says, "You have the right to talk to a lawyer and to have a lawyer with you while you are being questioned." The arrested person has a right to be *represented.*

A suspect makes his first appearance in front of a judge.

Law & Order Facts

Miranda Rights
1. You have the right to remain silent.
2. Anything you say can and will be used against you in a court of law.
3. You have the right to talk to a lawyer and have him present with you while you are being questioned.
4. If you cannot afford to hire a lawyer, one will be appointed to represent you before any questioning if you wish.
5. You can decide at any time to exercise these rights and not answer any questions or make any statements.

A lawyer may help the arrested person understand his or her rights and what to do in court. If an arrested person cannot pay for a lawyer, the state will assign one for free. This lawyer is called a **public defender**.

An accused person has the right to a *fair trial.* A fair trial is one that is decided on the evidence only. An accused person has the right to a *speedy trial.* The person does not have to wait too long before the trial.

A bail bondsman helps you with money to get out of jail while you wait for trial.

When the accused person goes to the first appearance, the court cannot set an *excessive bond.* The amount of bail cannot be too large. This right helps protect the accused from being forced to stay in jail because he or she cannot pay to get out.

CHAPTER EIGHT

RIGHTS OF THE VICTIM

Crime victims also have rights that help them bring the criminals to justice. A victim has the right to tell the police about a crime. Anybody can ask the police for help following a crime. The police may arrest the suspect if they have good reason. Victims also have the right to go to the accused person's trial. They are allowed to watch as the court decides whether the accused is guilty.

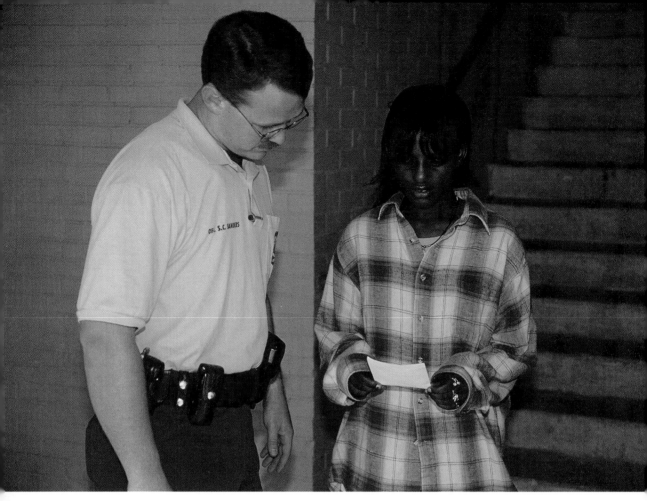

A law enforcement officer answers a young adult's questions.

Victims have the right to go to the sentencing of a guilty person. They can watch as a judge says how the criminal will be punished.

Victims sometimes have a right to **restitution**. Restitution is money paid to a victim by the criminal to make up for the crime. Restitution is usually part of a criminal's sentence. Victims also have the right to sue a criminal for damages.

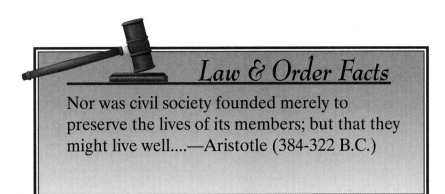

Criminals who damage a person's property are often made by the court to pay for the damage. If a criminal hurts someone, he or she may be made to pay the victim's medical bills. Sometimes criminals are made to pay victims for *pain and suffering.* This money is for the terrible experience the criminal forced upon the victim.

Prevention helps protect victims' rights. Many crimes can be prevented before they happen. The police can help prevent crimes by patrolling certain areas, and people can help by putting burglar alarms in their homes and cars, for example.

Education, too, can help prevent crimes. Everybody can learn basic safety rules like being careful after dark and avoiding strangers. In the past, victims' rights did not get noticed as much as they do now. Today our society always looks for better ways to protect the rights of innocent people.

GLOSSARY

amendment (uh MEND ment) — a change or addition to the U.S. Constitution

appeal (uh PEEL) — request for a new hearing in a court of law

arrest (uh REST) — seize and hold a person by authority of law

bail (BAYL) — money paid for the release of an arrested person as a promise that the person will appear for trial

bicameral (by KAM er ul) — made of two parts, especially of two lawmaking bodies

bill (BIL) — proposed law given to lawmakers for their approval

civil law (SIV ul LAW) — laws of a state or nation dealing with the rights of private citizens, not with crime and punishment

convict (KUN VIKT) — find or prove someone guilty of a crime, also (KAHN VIKT) a person found guilty of an offense or crime

court (KAWRT) — person or group whose task is to hear and decide court cases

criminal law (KRIM uh nul LAW) — laws that deal with public violent crimes and punishment for them

GLOSSARY

extradite (EK struh DYT) — turn over an accused person to the court that has power over him or her

federal court (FED er ul KAWRT) — court that makes decisions for the U.S. Government

justice (JUS tis) — fairness; also the steps for carrying out laws in the courts

Miranda rights (muh RAN duh RYTS) — five rights held by all accused persons; the rights to remain silent and to have a lawyer present when questioned

no contest (NO KON TEST) — plea of neither *guilty* nor *not guilty,* usually treated as a guilty plea by courts

plea (PLEE) — answer of guilty, not guilty or no contest, of an accused person to a criminal charge or indictment.

public defender (PUB lik di FEND r) — lawyer hired by a state to represent an accused person unable to pay for a lawyer

restitution (RES ti TOO shun) — act of returning something that was taken away

FURTHER READING

Find out more with these helpful books and information sites:

- Brown, Lawrence. *The Supreme Court.* Washington, DC: Congressional Quarterly, 1981.
- Conklin, John E. *Criminology.* Allyn and Bacon: Needham Heights, MA, 1995.
- De Sola, Ralph. *Crime Dictionary.* New York: Facts on File, 1988.
- Hill, Gerald and Hill, Kathleen. *Real Life Dictionary of the Law.* Los Angeles: General Publishing Group, 1995.
- Janosik, Robert, ed. *Encyclopedia of the American Judicial System.* New York: Charles Scribner and Sons, 1987.
- Johnson, Loch K. *America's Secret Power (CIA).* Oxford: OUP, 1989.
- Kadish, Sanford H., ed. *Encyclopedia of Crime and Justice.* New York: The Free Press, 1983.
- McShane, M. and Williams, F., eds. *Encyclopedia of American Prisons.* New York: Garland, 1996.
- Morris, N. and Rothman, D., eds. *The Oxford History of the Prison.* Oxford: OUP, 1995.
- Regoli, Robert and Hewitt, John. *Criminal Justice.* Prentice-Hall: Englewood Cliffs, NJ, 1996.
- Renstrum, Peter G. *The American Law Dictionary.* Santa Barbara, CA: ABC-CLIO, 1991.
- Territo, Leonard and others. *Crime & Justice in America.* West: St. Paul, MN, 1995.
- *The Constitution of the United States.* Available in many editions.
- *The Declaration of Independence.* Available in many editions.
- Voigt, Linda and others. *Criminology and Justice.* McGraw-Hill: New York, 1994.

- http://entp.hud.gov/comcrime.html
  Crime Prevention
  Department of Justice
  PAVNET (Partnership Against Violence Network)
  Justice Information Center
  Justice for Kids & Youth
- http://www.dare-america.com/
  Official Website of D.A.R.E.
- http://www.fightcrime.com/lcrime.htm
  Safety and Security Connection
  The Ultimate Guide to Safety and Security
  Resources on the Internet
- http://www.psrc.com/lkfederal.html
  Links to most Federal Agencies

INDEX